The Gift of Time

Written by Jean Tolfa Hansen
Illustrated by Jill Tolfa

Dear Dr Borovich,
Thank you for sharing your time and talent with me. Take time to smell the daffodils!
Fondly, Jean Hansen

Art Directors: Susan Lucas and Hannah Hansen

Images by Jill Tolfa

Published by Dog Ear Publishing
8888 Keystone Crossing, Suite 1300
Indianapolis, IN 46264
www.dogearpublishing.net

dog ear PUBLISHING

ISBN: 978-145757-020-9
Library of Congress Control Number: 2019906278

This book is printed on acid free paper.
Printed in the United States of America

Auntie

for Mollie and Hannah
Always and forever I will keep you
in my heart!

Mom

All the tiny caterpillars crept in a line.

Buttercup, a curious one, always lagged behind.

She stopped to smell the daffodils and watch the world go by.
She was in no hurry to become a butterfly.

One night, the caterpillars rushed to make their fine cocoons.

All except for Buttercup,

who stopped to wish upon the moon.

"I am not yet ready to hurry on my way.
I need time to learn, to discover, and to play!"

Because her heart was earnest, she found to her delight,
her wish was heard and granted by Star Fairies of the night.

The Star Fairies guided their tiny friend with love.

Mysteries of the world revealed through kindness from above.

High in the starry heavens, they watched her from afar.
The wind held their whispers, "You will always be our star!"

The end of spring was near and Buttercup felt strange.

The fairies gently told her, "It is time for you to change."

They sprinkled her with stardust as she began to weave.

They knew once she emerged, it was time for her to leave.

The chrysalis shook...

...and Buttercup broke free.

She spread her wings in awe and said,

"Take a look at me!"

She joined the other butterflies to flitter and fly around.
She fluttered in the sky and soared high above the ground.

Later in the evening, when the moon began to lift,

she thanked the Star Fairies for their very special gift.

"I know you will watch over me and we will never be apart,

because always and forever I will keep you in my heart!"

The End

CPSIA information can be obtained
at www.ICGtesting.com
Printed in the USA
BVHW061603041019
560082BV00021BA/269/P

9 781457 570209